Golden Universe

ELIZABETH ELSEY

WITH DRAWINGS BY
JORDAN UNDERWOOD

authorHOUSE®

AuthorHouse™
1663 Liberty Drive
Bloomington, IN 47403
www.authorhouse.com
Phone: 1 (800) 839-8640

Published by AuthorHouse 02/28/2018

ISBN: 978-1-5462-3170-7 (sc)
ISBN: 978-1-5462-3169-1 (e)

Print information available on the last page.

Any people depicted in stock imagery provided by Getty Images are models, and such images are being used for illustrative purposes only.
Certain stock imagery © Getty Images.

This book is printed on acid-free paper.

Because of the dynamic nature of the Internet, any web addresses or links contained in this book may have changed since publication and may no longer be valid. The views expressed in this work are solely those of the author and do not necessarily reflect the views of the publisher, and the publisher hereby disclaims any responsibility for them.

Dedicated to
any and all people with feeling

To the lovers
To the ones who are "over-emotional"
To the cries you let out at 3 am
To the blade dragged across your skin
To the stars
To the teachers
To the heartbreakers
To the trips we never got to take
To the A+ you never got
To the lost nights
To the tarot cards
To the trial and error
To the bullies
To the friends
To the cats and dogs
To the ten different homes
To those who felt the collapse and got back up
To the sun
To the moon
To the doubt
To my 2016 love
To you

Thank you.

Heart

Flying

I fell in love, I dove deep
with magic pearls and mercury.
Rays of sun shone through my pores
cleaning out my unloved, unwanted
dirt.

I fell in love with angels
that manifested in my car
window in Chicago wind.
I'm never tired of that drive,
love.

Your voice versed the aux cord
in my favorite battle on
technology I've ever heard.
And when your voice rang out, I flew
gold.

I Am My Own

Your control was never enough to love me.
Your love was never enough to keep me.

Mental Abuse

When they tell you they'll die without you
how could you ever choose your happiness over that?
Often times, you don't.

Flowers

I once thought a girl was my soulmate
because she could make candles in my favorite
scent.
I didn't know that she could also
make a fire in my brain
that crackled so loud
it broke my thoughts.

Overgrown Branch

The problem with hopeless
romantics is that we
think everyone is
the love of our life. And
once that seed is planted
the tree only grows, through
our lungs, fills our throats, and
creates the words that force
themselves out over and over.

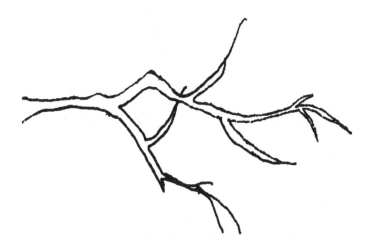

A.M

When you asked me
how this made me feel
I said this feels like winning the lottery
because I feel like I can do anything.

Moon

I wanted to watch the sun rise with you
but when I looked beside me
you had already set.

Timing

I didn't want to face this poem,
to realize it didn't work out,
that the cosmos are screaming at us.
But they fucked up their schedule,
and it's too late.

For Never

Being in love with you
felt like the first thing I did really well.
felt like the first thing I didn't fuck up.
I wrote you forever
in a shredded notebook;
I built you sand castles out of cement;
I made you crystals out of torment;
I sang you glitter
with voice covered in shards of glass;
I grew you warmth
from the freezing cold rain;
until I realized
I never really
mattered.

And I guess even the airplanes
that fly so high all come down
eventually.
And I crashed.
I became the dust too.
And I was so mad
when I finally got back in my head.
I was good to you.
I gave you chances,
more than two,
and I should've stopped at one.

But you know,
you were the second thing in my life
to ever give me a purpose.
The first was a little girl,
with the same mother as me,
who smiles like she has the stars in her teeth.
And I thought you'd give me those stars on a string,
to wear around my neck.
But it turns out you were giving them to another girl
to wear around her heart
and I found out on Valentine's Day.
It's fine.
Hearts and candy and cupid
are all stupid anyway.
Your love was an unfortunate cycle,
a black heart in a beast too old to care,
or feel;
your love was a never ending target practice
for arrows with the cute red hearts.
That love wasn't a folded up card
with a candy taped to it;
that love was a folded up heart
with a dagger stabbed in the back
and twisted just enough to make me the puppet.
You
used
me,
to make your broken relationship with someone else
fixed
and better.
So while I fell in love, you fell into my words

and stole them to use on someone else.
I am not a band-aid, I
am not a fireman to come get your
broken dreams out of a tree.

So here's your sheath
full of all the arrows shot at me
by that delusional baby in a diaper.
They don't work anymore.
And neither do we.

Voicemail

Press 1 for I never want to see you again.
I never want to feel your grin against my face.
I never want to miss your hands again.
I never want to feel your hips between my legs.

Press 2 for you never really loved me anyway.
I was a temporary solution to your temporary emotion.

Press 3 for crying in the shower on the bathtub floor.
I don't want to know how much of the water is my tears
or the water coming from the drain.

Press 4 for I want you back.
But I don't want you back.
But I do want you back.
But I don't
want you
back.
But I do.
But I'm a mess but I'm not a mess.
But I want my home back.

Press 5 for not feeling anything at all
I haven't eaten in two weeks;
I haven't smiled since Thursday;
I haven't even cried.
I think I lost my tears down the drain.

Press 6 if you'd like to speak to my best friend.
She'll kill you.
And then she'll come back
to tell me if she left bruises on you
worse than the ones on my heart.

Press 7 for future me,
to hear if she's doing okay.
Call me back and let me know.
Right now it doesn't feel like that's possible

Press 8 for my assistant,
my brain.
We don't listen to her very often.
My heart is the boss,
and it's in a time out right now.

Press 9 for my healing
It's a very slow message but
maybe it'll tell you I made it.

Otherwise you may hang up.
There are no other options.

———ᴠᴠᴏᴏᴏᴏᴏᴏᴏᴏᴏᴠᴠ———

Absent

Even when I was with you
I might as well have been living without you.

Moving On

I am losing,
leaf after
leaf and still,
I can grow.

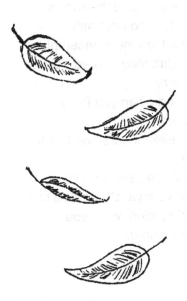

Seven

Winter has never been so cold.
You left me with nothing to pour out.
At least everyone else,
they gave me purpose.
Was it because the icicles
that I formed from ash
still had too much resemblance
of the fire they burned from?
I'm sorry
I burned when you froze.
I'm sorry
you never understood that love
is fire.
I think I can still remember
when your words created sparks.
But they died when you
gave up on us.

Process

Raining
Chasing
Fighting
Lost

Hesitating
Raining
Giving
Lost

Backtracking
Pouring
Winning
Lost

Knocked down
Crawling
Rising
Walking
Running

Crying

Fighting
Crying
Hoping
Searching
Finding
Winning

Learning
Falling
Smiling
Flying

Healing

The Physics and The Sweetner

It was never just about sex.
Maybe that first night it was.
Maybe it was about the excitement,
curiosity of a new tune,
and we couldn't stop singing it.

But even the sex was too passionate,
too electric, too *baby i need
your hair between my fingers,*
too fitting to just call it sex.

I can't even say
it was making love
because we did that every time our eyes met,
and the browns mixed,
just as much as our bodies ever could.

So we became more than the physical touch,
we became the energy around us,
the fire in our words.
The laugh of children that filled our lungs,
we became every fiber
of that blanket, every line to our playlist.
She brought those sexy eyebrows
to the parking lot of the mall,
the first place I heard her whisper,

"Can I kiss you?"
And our waterfall started,
and found that the sex was only step one.

A few weeks later,
she built me a gift basket of Hershey Kisses and told me
have these when I'm not here.
She bought me a nail polish called "significant other
color" and said
Baby look how pretty.
I wore that sparkly purple iridescence for a week,
until my fingertips painted red and blue.

She's as messy as the smudge she leaves on my
glasses
every damn time she kisses me.
But I'm a neat freak and she
will always be the mess I love to clean.
The mess I love to create,
when my hands touch her soft skin
and we make a mess with the tension,
and then with the lips.
And I live for these moments
when the cacoa trees shiver in envy
knowing we can become more sweet than they ever will.
And I'll always grow,
make a mess
clean it up,
if it means her life will be a little sweeter

Tidal Wave

Be the beauty
that has the strength to protect
but also to hold me softly.
Don't let the world turn you
into rough sand and dirt.
The galaxies in your ocean
keep me mesmerized forever.

Bookstore Love Story

She proposed to me on a bench.
The same bench where we kissed that day
and that day
it was very clear,
we wanted only each other.
Now when I look
at the glossed over wood,
I can only see
love
and white sapphires.
Surrounded by pages of love stories,
surrounded by books,
and she will always be
my favorite bookstore love story.

---wwoɔ⭕ɔ⭕ɔ⭕ɔowm---

I Know It's Not Your Fault

I know you aren't the owner of this newly healed scar
on my heart.
But I'm afraid and I think I always will be.
Just promise you won't tear it open again.

Angel Dust

In July, you told me
you love stained glass.
I spent the rest of that month
finding the glass pieces to my heart
and coloring them just right
so when the summer sun shone through me
I'd be your angel.
By the beginning of August,
angel dust filled our bodies,
and those glass colors inside me glowed.
I was your chapel, and baby, you
you were my priest,
reading me verse after verse,
making me scream to the universe:
This is where I want to be, God,
if I am an angel
from these broken glass pieces,
then I am hers and hers forever.
Because only her kaleidoscope eyes
can appreciate my wings.
And I am this stained glass angel
because of her.

Blue

June 12th

It has been 7 months,
1 week,
and 4 days
since I met your soul.
Not since I saw your body
and the way it moves like an ocean,
but since I saw you cry
in the driver's seat of your car,
and I saw your mind open
like a four lane highway after rush hour.

I saw your brown eyes turn blue
at the words *you're trying your best.*
And it wasn't your body but your mind that undressed.
It was the curtain of a room that dropped like fog in a
forest,

And you were my oak tree growing beside me,
widening a trunk big enough to store our love,
and lift it up through the branches when we smile,
with leaves that touch the sky as softly as our lips did
on the bench in the bookstore
where we first learned the strength of our love.

I was a kite,
and you were the string,
keeping me from dashing too close to the sun,
protecting my thin skin,
keeping me from getting burned
even though the only thing I feel
when my lips touch your skin
is fire.

So baby, I want those tears gone.
I want you to know that you're always trying your best,
with my hand against your chest to feel your breath,
calming my anxiety. Your best
always makes my waves stop crashing,
makes my heart still grow and keeps yours still glowing.

So that by the end, your driver's seat is still the driver's
seat.
And those tears are not tears, they are a wish
that our tree
will still grow.

Hold Me

I want my smile to live
forever against your lips.

Peridot

You're the best constellation in my night sky.
You're the melting snow in my depression winter,
making sure there's still flowers
because you know they make me smile,
help me breathe.
You're the breathing.

Beauty Marks

This journey started with Spider-Man,
his intricate webs.
He spun webs and we dove into
the intricacy of our built walls.
Those bricks are not simple.
We have trust issues, humans do.
Your heart broke by the hands
of self-esteems biggest flaws,
and I was thrown
off path by lies
hiding behind the face of love
and here we came together
connected like connect-the-dots, but with stars.
And baby, you're made of stars.
For god's sake, you have the Big Dipper
outlined in beauty marks on your right arm
and I want to create the sky for you.
Come home to that,
grow in that,
deeper,
and deeper.
Dark parts aren't forever,
save that for the night sky, lover.
Focus on the intricacy, please.
Never forget where we started.
Fighting the venom,

burning in fire,
lie in my sand.
Let me hold you.
Octopus,
intricate,
complicated,
science,
love,
romance.
It's not that simple anymore.
We are not kids,
this is not a playground, we
are not imagining the web, it's in us.
We are the intricacy
Lover
I'll never say that your battles with the villains are small
I know full well they tear your buildings down
and put holes in the windows. We're adults now,
I'm sorry, but it's true.
That means our battles
are real now, not a show
Tobey McGuire can't fight them all.
But I'm here,
I swear,
I'm here,
to fix your suit,
to hold you.
I promise
you don't have to listen
to that police radio every second.
Give yourself rest,

sleep
on our stars.
This intricacy is not a curse,
it is so beautiful.
This journey
is so
beautiful.

To-Do List

Laughing with you
will always be
the most important thing to do today.

Apple

I can't wait
to watch your flowers
grow through the scratches
in your heart,
to watch your infinity grow
into a garden of healed pain,
and see you as a the brightest red.

Fight

Black is a veil
Red is a mouth
Purple is a bruise
Yellow is the healing

Women

We will always be the strongest force anyone could ever imagine.

Growth

Please be better than I am.
It means the world is getting smarter.

The Rocket

Yesterday
I bought a rainbow flag sticker
from a toy store in Ypsilanti.

Today, I look at its centric placement
on the front of my laptop,
and I realize I'm no longer afraid.

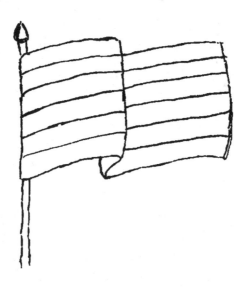

Underdogs

I haven't stood for the National Anthem since 7th grade,
when I realized our liberty means shooting the innocent
until their guilty is forced through.
And the justice for all
was a finish line
way down the path, not the truth.
In 12th grade I realized
I forgot the words.

Because pledging my allegiance under God just
isn't my style,
and isn't my faith.

And I will not stand
holding my beloved heart
chanting like a brainwashed dummy
to a country run by people who swear by the Bible
but do not understand it.

Because my religious father,
who was the most understanding
about my sexuality
out of everyone I knew,
he vowed to make my wedding dress when I married a
woman,
rather than refuse to make a cake.

I will not stand
for an anthem that goes against my people,

most people.
I will not pretend
that what we see on the television every day
is called freedom.
Because I had this teacher,
in 11th grade,
who taught me what the world used to be,
so I know
where we came from, who we are.
This is not what America stands for,
we know that. You
know that. So
I'll wait out this apocalypse.
Wait, no, I'll fight this damn apocalypse.
I will kneel with Kaepernick,
speak like Ellen,
learn like Michelle,
march with my words in my back pocket like Halsey,
I won't just wait, this National Anthem will see it's finish
line.
So I know we'll fight,
straight-faced, hands clenched.
Underdogs
with the rest of us.

AR-15

Someday
it'll be a more impressive feat
for kids to name the ever changing top 20
of America's mass shootings
than all of its states or its presidents.

Remember

I am so sorry
you had to leave a world
because people care more about guns
than children.
I am so sorry
you were buried in a box
that should not have been made so soon.

We Change

I used to plan out what I would do in the zombie apocalypse.
I'd steal a bus, and drive around town to pick up everyone I could.
As I've gotten older, the list of people to pick up has grown.
But so has the list of people I'm convinced are too late to save.

2016 Election

I spoke my fear for the future,
where we were headed and how
all our hope felt blown away, out of reach.

My grandmother once said she wants to live
long enough to see her grandchildren get married.
And I was worried I might never be able to.

She told me, "Don't give up,
this is only a setback."

Grandma, I won't give up.

The Earth

Watching you burn,
hearing you crash,
knowing your golden wooden trees
and sparkling, pure seas
are poisoned
is always the heaviest weight on my chest.
Beauty only exists because of you
and your eternal spin, your eternal sun,
over and over.
Your rule over everyone,
but your constant choice not to use it,
is the best teacher for patience.
Your surface is huge
but never have you been called fat or ugly,
and your rolls create mountains
worthy of the softest kisses.
I will always stand beside you, knowing
what we've done is not what you deserve,
and I can't give much but my words
to praise you and say you are loved.

Stay Smart

You'll outnumber the bad guys
with intelligence fierce as mountains.
This generation is not lazy.

To the Proud Bisexual Who Wore A "Gay and Here to Stay" Shirt to a Pride Festival

Do you know how many people
fight to be seen every day?
How many people want to be proud
of who they are, like you?
There are so many who are erased, ignored, and walked over
because people like you
hide behind a fake label.
There are people who are oppressed at this very festival
by their own people, and I'm sure you know,
some people don't even believe bisexuality exists.
There are people afraid to come out because of this climate.
And in a place where this is supposed to be celebrated,
you and all your pride
chose a gay shirt,
proving even more how the biggest part of the LGBT community
is oppressed.
If you have pride for who you are
please show it.
You're not confused or a cheater
or privileged because you can "move back and forth"
and I know you are proud.
Show the kids that you are not the Silent Majority.

Don't be silent.
Do you understand the significance of the color purple?
To some kids, it's the only color they want to see
and they can't.
Be the example that shows
purple is the most beautiful color,
and that the only phase going on here
is that shirt.

Breaking the Rules

I always made sure I had matching socks.
My mom told me to.
I could never figure out how to fold a pair together,
so I made her do it for me.
But all that mattered was that they matched

I noticed the girl across the street
did not follow the same rules,
and she didn't seem to care.
One was yellow and one was pink.
And from that day on I realized
matching socks didn't matter

I guess that was my first time breaking the rules.
One day
I went in the cupboard for the bag of M&Ms.
I dropped the bag
and the candy scattered everywhere,
and was not at all quiet.
My sweet tooth was born from that drop.

Teen years, it spread to graffiti
on the giant poles under the bridge.
Sneaking a carton of milk from the lunch line,
cheating on tests, copying answers, doing other
people's homework.
Subtle paint wars under the desk in art class.
It made life more colorful anyway

Speaking out of turn was breaking the rules,
not raising my hand was breaking the rules,
being too loud sent me up to the teacher's desk,
singing in choir when my section wasn't supposed to sing,
stealing music when we were supposed to give it back,
because I just wanted to remember the song.

I kept talking when even my friends told me to stop,
if it meant I was standing up for myself.
It turns out those mismatching socks brought me
somewhere better.
Not jail.

It brought me to confidence
It brought me to fun
It gave me every opportunity I would've missed
otherwise
to look back on childhood and say
I had fun.

I sat down when it wasn't something I wanted to
stand for;
I stood up when it was absolutely something I wanted
to stand for.
And believe me I stood alone a lot;
I stood when I wasn't supposed to
A lot.

I'm still a good friend,
a sister,
a girlfriend,
a student,
a kid

I'm still
good.

Society

We are an open
mind, a radiant
combination of
millions of brains.
And you filled us with
corruption.

We wanted a life
of rightful earnings
and happy success.

But we got pounded,
and prodded. Until
we lost our open
mind, open heart too.
Open idea
to everything
we could have done for
the world but you - you
closed it. You locked it.

You let the broken
children cry and beg.
You watched, as cities
fell and covered our
faces in dust and

despair and nothing
is left now, but you
don't care. You felt it
for no time at all.

And,
I'm afraid of you.

———*~~∽∾*∽∾———

Family

———*~~∽∾*∽∾———

——⁓ww⁓◦◦⁓⁓◦◦⁓◦ww——

Mother

The smell of lavender
will never hold a candle to you.

In the World

When I was born, my grandpa
popped open a bottle of champagne
in the hallway outside the door.
I think I heard the pop from the room I was in.
Because in my head I hear celebration
all the time
behind doors I can't wait to open.

October 2nd, 2012

Never has something so small
given me the biggest reason to love.

Cells

You have millions of little tiny things
trying to keep you alive every day.
They work and fight constantly
making sure you're okay.
You'll never have a better supporter
than your own body.

Grandmother

Thank you for showing me
that a story is the best thing to tell.
That words have meaning,
on a page, and reading,
of all kinds,
is so important.

—ᴡᴡ◦ᴄᴇ✿ᴏᴋᴇ◦ᴏᴡᴡ—

Soft

—ᴡᴡ◦ᴄᴇ✿ᴏᴋᴇ◦ᴏᴡᴡ—

You will make it.

She is

Comparison
will tear you down
more than she ever will.

Extrovert with Anxiety

I want to talk to you but
I need to talk to you but
I need interaction but
my heart rate says otherwise and
I walk away.

Better Now

About a year ago,
I asked the moon to take me away.
It didn't take me but I think it took the sadness.
And now "me" has a different meaning.

Older

When I was a kid, the world used to darken when I stepped into it.
As an adult, I know the world gets dark sometimes but will eventually get lighter.

God

It feels like these scars were from cuts I had to discover
myself
to learn all that I had inside of me
before I could heal myself back up and walk
knowing what I am fully capable of.

Music

I want to cover myself in
all the lyrics that
made me feel more like a person than
my own body ever did.

Voices

I shut down when someone gets too loud.
I run away.

My panic attacks,
they don't happen outside.
They happen inside,
harmonizing all those voices.

I once had a panic
over telling her "I love you."
over not being able to say it.
But the voices told me I needed to.

I'm scared of reusable water bottles.
Also of the top stair in a staircase;
I'm scared my weight will tip the whole thing over.

I'm scared of people with facial hair,
as if each prickly hair is a blade,
and I'm very aware of my thin skin.

I feel safer walking at night than day.
I feel like the stars will keep me safe,
but the sun will just attack me.
And I carry my pocket knife,
from my dad,

in my hand walking down the Detroit streets in broad
daylight.
Not always night.

Would you rather travel deep space or deep ocean?
Deep ocean because the never ending open space
scares me.
Needles scare me but I have 10 tattoos.
It's better than the doctors office.

It's not the cold hands or the rubber gloves,
it's the constant thought of *today, somehow, I could find
out I have cancer.*
I'm a hypochondriac.
I'm almost always afraid I'm sick.

I'm aware of these issues.

See, I am constantly a moving ocean.
I'm moving in a space between all of this,
the beating red chest on top of me,
the smile covering the words they speak.

These teeth show I should calm down and take it.
They'll say I'm sensitive,
for letting words cut into me like knives,
even songs
rip my heart and spill quick heart beats.
And I can't listen to the radio because
I am sensitive. Always.

My chest will always be broken open and ready
for jabs, and it hurts. But I can't close it.
I try, with my toolbox of "you are strong"

to toughen my skin, break those knives, become
acceptable.

I could have been something.
A member of the board of education
could have saved kids,
saved animals from cages.
I could have been something apart from this heart.

An astronaut could
land on new planets.
A mathematician,
anything better than
a broken psyche
devised by laws of deep depression,
a spiral of dark green hues,
killed
and reborn
every morning
by those yellow, sparks of madness that attack me
and they climb,
through my damn window.
And this ugly lime green color kills me.

So why is the only thing I'm capable
of achieving
in this body
is madly neutral,
frightening screams for peace of mind?

I'm not a vessel
for this tormented mind.

But here I am.
And I could have been so much.

But I wanted to
be torn.

Anxiety

These shakes
are from
the unexplained fear
of nothing.
I can't get in a full breath.

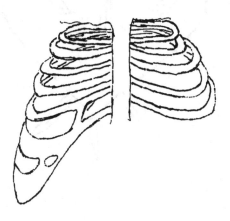

Sapphire

Since birth I've embodied impossible
and sometimes you look at me
like I'm the most impossible you've
ever seen.
But I promise there's no one
more fit to solve my puzzle than you.
Please don't lose my pieces.
Don't let me lose my pieces.

New Year's Broken List

Every year for as long as I can remember
I have written "lose weight" on my new year's resolution list.
It's been four years and I can still see
the word "pain" as a scar on my leg
from when I carved it at sixteen years old
with the hope that it would start a chain reaction
and the rest of me would peel off.

My ex once told me I should go to therapy
so I can learn that my weight isn't the end of the world.
Any "fat girl" will tell you, sir, that our weight
absolutely is the end of the world.
Every time we eat, it feels like we're eating the world
and it's ending inside of us.

No one looks at the Grand Canyon and thinks
that it's fat.
They look at it and think, that is
beautiful.
And that thing is damn near 300 miles long.
It's huge.

Huge.
A word I'm all too familiar with.
A word I'm a little worried I'll never grow out of,
or rather, shrink out of.

But don't worry, everyone has rolls when they bend over.

But do everyone's rolls look like last night's dinner I
convinced myself I didn't need?
Do everyone's rolls look like the disappointment in
myself?
Or the disappointment in my family's eyes when they ask
if I've put on weight?
I am tired
of looking at pictures from my childhood and asking
myself
what went wrong?
I am tired
of every new year being another season to beg my body
to finally just listen,
to beg my body to finally just peel away.

One day my fiancée told me she's considered morbidly
obese,
according to multiple charts found on the internet,
and I couldn't help but think *honey*
you are anything but morbid
and if you are morbidly anything
you are morbidly perfect.
One day I watched
when she got out of the shower
and came into the bedroom wearing
nothing but boxers and I thought
what a blessing it is that this masterpiece
takes up so much space.

Honey,
I want to be spacious.

This Other World

Outside;
They see a face,
my soft features but eyes,
sharp as razors. A body,
skin, white as frost, never
taken off guard.
You can never
make me vulnerable.
I'll know how to protect
myself. My mountains will always guard me.

Inside;
What they don't see,
a chest full of ribs, caging
a muscle strong as diamond
instructing a maze of veins
controlled by a skull.
A universe, an ocean, a
beautiful combination of
everything and anything the
cosmos could ever create.
A miracle and a masterpiece.

My stars are ice; my
mountains are blades;
my sky - my thoughts - comes off as

cotton candy
but inside is a different hue.
And I don't want to die without
ever being understood by you.
I don't want to die
without ever being seen.

Depression

I can't tell if I think the sun is my savior
or the demon mocking me for not resembling it.

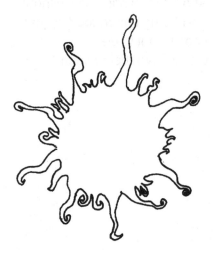

Bed

Get up,
brush that dust off.
the kind that the tears left;
the kind that the screams left
from a war never won but rather paused.

You have to get up
with nothing to feel,
no fear because you know it,
no worry because it's too late.
But with nothing to feel,
you have everything to fight with.

I know the world has already gone dull;
vibrancy isn't in your vocabulary anymore.
But i've never seen dull colors
without an artist waiting to destroy it
holding a palette of the world's brightest.

So on those nights, morning,
days, whatever, whenever,
that your hands are stained red
know that someone
out there
is trying to make the world brighter
and you'll always make their palette better.

Curves

I loved you because you were the first person
to love my body instead of my mind.
Because it hurts
going through life
having people tell you how smart
or creative you are
as a way to avoid the topic of your body.
Listen, I get that my shadow
is bigger than everyone else's
but the lost boys can still follow my lead.
I've got enough scars already.
One on my leg is called
"That time John from 4th grade
called me wooly mammoth
and it stuck."
and the other one
right next to it is called,
"Always getting picked last in gym class."
Most of the rest are called,
"All the times people said *is she cute?*
Well she's funny."
Yeah. I get it.
I get that I can't run that mile.
I get that she was thinner than me
so of course you took her to the dance.
I get that I've been this way my whole life.

I get the jokes; I've heard them all.
I get that I was the slowest on the softball team.

But there's this girl
who laid me down on her bed and looked at me
like I was the MV-fucking-P,
like I made every home run,
like she would've taken me to every dance,
every date, every fucking team in gym class
that I wasn't picked for,
like a wooly mammoth is her favorite animal,
like she thinks I'm cute and laughs at my jokes.
And when she looks at me
and her eyes sparkle like a chocolate labrador when
their person comes home
I swear, I
am
home.
And my curves aren't the punchline
for your stupid jokes.
They're the part of me that she hugs
to make me feel whole.

Psychology

Your roots
are in my veins .
You are my history,
my cells keeping me alive.
Your past is my past.
Where you come from
is what keeps me alive.

Cunning Beauty

I want to wait each night
until the sky catches up with my mood.
But night is not where I am.
Dark nights have a richness,
a texture,
a story, and
a sort of cunning beauty.
They have an attitude
and a confidence.
They have a thick, dark masterpiece aura.
I'm the cloudy, silent fog,
the day-time dreary
of sun that tries but
can't make it through the clouds
because the clouds are too much.
I'm the neutral silence
that leaves the day
gray.
I'm not dark with the voice of stars.
I am too gray, almost light, but too cloudy
to see the sun.
A different kind of night.

Talking to the Universe When You're Alone

Become friends with the stars and know that they'll protect you. Look for them on those nights that your mind lights on fire. Understand that they are part of you, and that you're created from them. They'll make sure you're okay.

Absorb the dark night, as a hummingbird absorbs sugar. Feel it in your bones like you feel your best friend's laugh. Understand the bruise that sorrow kicked into your heart, and open that up to the sky. Let it put that sorrow at ease.

Appreciate the moon's beauty, and know she isn't conceited. Understand her selflessness. Repeat her cycles and renew yourself. Ask her how she's even more elegant each time.

Sometimes there are storms, the kind that darken every corner of your house but expose the sky in bright bolts. They're the kind of storms that you feel inside you right before they break, the kind that threaten the trees to fall down over top of you. Know it's just the ground and the clouds talking out their problems. Ask them how their conversations are so intelligent that they light up the sky and put on a show.

Get to know the planets, their differences and their sizes. Diversity creates the galaxy.

Learn the mistakes of the black holes, how they turned in on themselves from beautiful stars. They caved in, and took everything with them. Make sure you don't ask them too many questions. Don't let yourself cave in.

Talk to the universe; it will always be there. Learn that you'll never be alone.

Printed in the United States
By Bookmasters